London

Catriona Clarke

Designed by Tom Lalonde

Illustrated by Terry McKenna

London consultant: Hedley Swain, Museum of London
Reading consultant: Alison Kelly

Contents

This is London

London is the biggest city
in the United Kingdom.
It is also the
capital city.

This photo shows
London at sunset.

In the beginning

Over 2000 years ago there were just a few farms where London is now. Then the Romans arrived and built a big town called Londinium.

The Romans built a bridge so they could cross the river easily.

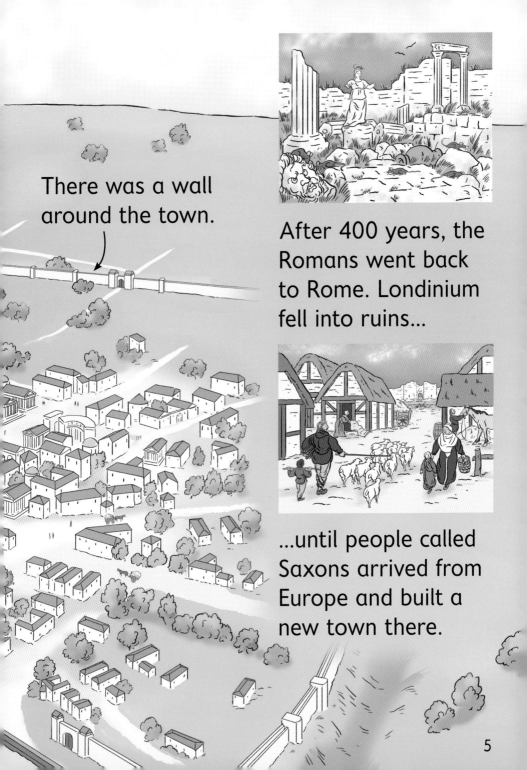

There was a wall around the town.

After 400 years, the Romans went back to Rome. Londinium fell into ruins...

...until people called Saxons arrived from Europe and built a new town there.

The Royals arrive

By the year 1065, London had become so important that a king decided to live there.

A king named Edward built an abbey and a palace just outside the city, at Westminster.

Since then, Westminster Abbey has been rebuilt and changed by lots of different kings.

Most kings and queens have been crowned in the Abbey, and buried there when they died.

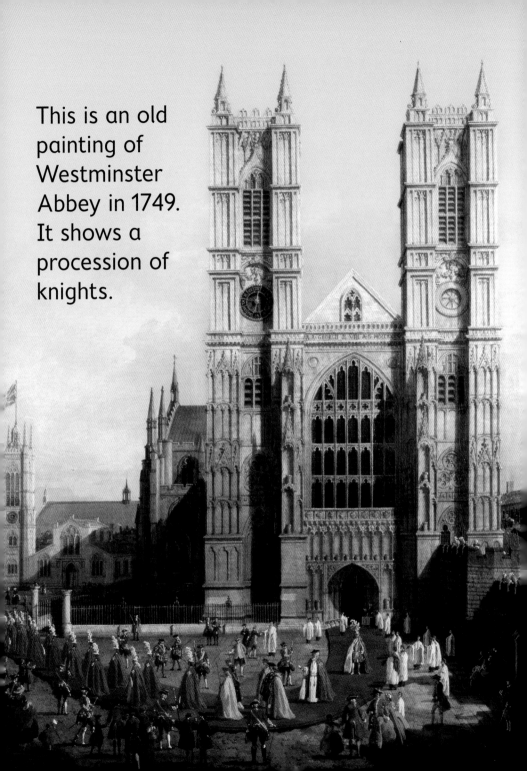

This is an old painting of Westminster Abbey in 1749. It shows a procession of knights.

Bridging the river

The River Thames was very important to London and the people who lived there.

People used water from the river for drinking, cooking and washing.

Ships from all over the world sailed up the river to London from the sea.

This painting shows London in 1630.

There were lots of small boats on the river.
People used these just like taxi cabs today.

These ships carried
lots of things such
as food, cloth and
exotic spices.

There was one bridge
across the river.
It had lots of shops
and houses along it.

The Tower

The Tower of London was built in 1078. Since then it's been a castle, a palace and a prison.

This is what it looked like 300 years ago.

It was the safest place in London, so the precious jewels and crowns that belonged to the king or queen were kept there.

A polar bear was once kept at the Tower.
It was allowed out to catch fish in the Thames!

Very important prisoners had their
heads chopped off at the Tower.

This picture shows Lady
Jane Grey just before
her execution.

Having fun

About 400 years ago, there were lots of different ways for Londoners to have fun.

Sometimes the Thames froze over in winter. People held frost fairs with stalls, games and horse racing on the icy river.

There were fairs in the summertime too, with food stalls, music and dancing.

The Globe Theatre was a famous playhouse where people watched plays.

The Great Plague

The plague was a deadly disease that had no cure. A terrible plague hit London in 1665. It killed thousands of people.

The plague was spread by fleas that lived on black rats.

Most rich people left London to escape the disease.

People who caught the plague were shut in their houses...

...so they couldn't spread the disease to anyone else.

Some poor people,
like this woman, died
in the street.

At the time, people thought cats
and dogs carried the plague, so
they killed them.

London's burning

In 1666 there was a massive fire that became known as the Great Fire of London.

The fire started one night at a bakery in Pudding Lane, near London Bridge.

The flames spread quickly because of the wooden buildings and strong winds.

This painting shows the view from the Thames as the fire was raging.

Even the king helped to fight the fire!

People blew up buildings to try to stop the fire from spreading...

...but it destroyed most of London and left thousands of people with no home.

Bigger and better

After the Great Fire, London had to be completely rebuilt. Over the next 100 years, the city grew faster than ever before.

Houses were built from brick and stone, so that fires wouldn't spread so easily.

The new streets were much wider than they had been before the Great Fire.

London became the biggest and richest city in the world.

There were
beautiful parks
called pleasure
gardens.

Rich people dressed in their finest clothes to visit the gardens.

Dirty!

150 years ago, the River Thames was filthy. It was full of waste and sewage.

The air was very dirty too. It was full of smoke from coal fires.

This painting shows the Houses of Parliament through the smog (smoke and fog).

Sometimes the smog was so thick that people couldn't even see their own feet!

Lots of people got nasty diseases by drinking water pumped from the Thames.

One summer, the smell of the river was so bad it was called 'The Great Stink'...

...so huge pipes called sewers were built to flush sewage straight out to sea.

Rich and poor

Life in London was very different for rich people and poor people.

Many poor people lived in dirty, cramped slums in the east of the city.

Lots of families lived together in one house, with one family in each room.

They shared a toilet outside.

Nursery

Maid's room

Drawing room

Dining room

Kitchen

Scullery

Rich people lived in big houses. They had lots of servants to look after them.

Some children as young as five years old had to sweep chimneys to earn money.

Going underground

As London became bigger and bigger, the roads got busier and busier. People needed a new way to get around.

There were trains, trams and buses...

...and then someone had the idea of building a railway under the ground.

A street was dug up and railway tracks were laid down.

Then a tunnel was built and the road was replaced.

This old photograph shows the first London Underground journey in 1863.

The carriages were open, so it was very smelly and smoky.

Today, there are many underground tunnels deep beneath London.

A city at war

In the Second World War, London was attacked by German bomber planes.

Most children went to stay with families in the countryside where it was safer.

People who stayed behind often sheltered from the bombs in the Underground.

Every night there was a 'blackout'. This meant that no lights were allowed...

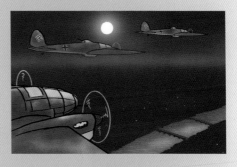

...so it was harder for the German pilots to see where to bomb.

This photograph shows St. Paul's Cathedral.

The smoke is from lots of bombs that fell nearby.

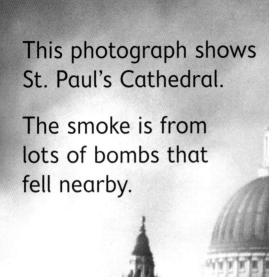

Many people were killed and lots of buildings were destroyed. This time was known as the 'Blitz'.

London today

Today, London is a bustling and exciting city of around nine million people.

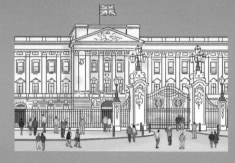

Oxford Street is one of the busiest shopping streets in Europe.

Buckingham Palace is one of the king's homes. Many tourists visit the palace.

This is the London skyline at night.

More than 300 different languages are spoken in London today.

Lots of people work in offices in tall buildings in a part of London called the City.

There are over 30 bridges across the Thames. This one is Tower Bridge.

Glossary

Here are some of the words in this book you might not know. This page tells you what they mean.

 Londinium - the name the Romans gave London 2000 years ago.

 River Thames - the wide river that flows through London.

 Globe Theatre - a playhouse that showed William Shakespeare's plays.

 plague - a terrible disease that kills lots of people.

 Houses of Parliament - the building where the Government meets.

 London Underground - the railway system that runs beneath London.

 the Blitz - the night-time bombing of London in the Second World War.

Usborne Quicklinks

Would you like to find out more about London and its history? You can visit Usborne Quicklinks for links to websites with videos, amazing facts and things to make and do.

Go to **usborne.com/Quicklinks** and type in the keywords "**beginners London**". Make sure you ask a grown-up before going online.

Notes for grown-ups

Please read the internet safety guidelines at Usborne Quicklinks with your child. Children should be supervised online. The websites are regularly reviewed and the links at Usborne Quicklinks are updated. However, Usborne Publishing is not responsible and does not accept liability for the content or availability of any website other than its own.

This is a guard outside Buckingham Palace. Soldiers from different regiments in the British Army guard the palace at different times.

Index

Acknowledgements

Photographic manipulation by Nick Wakeford and Will Dawes

Photo credits

The publishers are grateful to the following for permission to reproduce material:
Cover © Sven Hansche/EyeEm/Getty Images; **p1** © duncan1890/Digital Vision Vectors/Getty Images; **p2-3** © Douglas
Pearson/Photolibrary/Getty Images; **p7** © Artefact/Alamy Stock Photo; **p8-9, 12-13, 16-17** © Museum of London/
Heritage-Images; **p10** © Art Images/Hulton Fine Art Collection/Getty Images; **p11** © The Print Collector/Heritage-
Images; **p15** © Mary Evans Picture Library; **p19** © Bibliotheque des Arts Decoratifs, Paris, France/Archives Charmet/The
Bridgeman Art Library; **p20** © Pictures Now/Alamy Stock Photo; **p25** © Hulton Archive/Getty Images; **p27** © Shawshots/
Alamy Stock Photo; **p28-29** © Matt Mawson/Getty Images; **p31** © AM Stock 2/Alamy Stock Photo.

Every effort has been made to trace and acknowledge ownership of copyright. If any rights have
been omitted, the publishers offer to rectify this in any subsequent editions following notification.

Usborne Beginners
Sun, Moon and Stars

Usborne Beginners
Farm Animals

Katie Daynes
Illustrated by Christyan Fox

Elizabeth I

Usborne Beginners
Rubbish & Recycling

Stephanie Turnbull
Illustrated by Christyan Fox

Usborne Beginners
Dogs

Emma Helbrough
Illustrated by Nicholas Stevens

Usborne Beginners
Horses & Ponies

Anna Milbourne
Illustrated by Graziella Gazzmeni

Usborne Beginners
Cats

Usborne Beginners
Ancient Greeks

Stephanie Turnbull
Illustrated by Colin King

Usborne Beginners
Spiders

Usborne Beginners
VOLCANOES

Stephanie Turnbull
Illustrated by Andy Tudor

Usborne Beginners
DINOSAURS

Stephanie Turnbull
Illustrated by Tetsuo Koshi

Usborne Beginners
Your Body

Stephanie Turnbull
Illustrated by Adam Larkum

Usborne Beginners
Armour

Usborne Beginners
Sharks

Catriona Clarke
Illustrated by Adam Relf

Usborne Beginners
The Celts

Usborne Beginners
VIKINGS

Stephanie Turnbull
Illustrated by Adam Larkum

Usborne Beginners
Castles

Stephanie Turnbull
Illustrated by Colin King

Usborne Beginners
How flowers grow

Emma Helbrough
Illustrated by Maggie Silver

Usborne Beginners
Digging up the past

Emma Jane Gilmartin
Illustrated by Maria Cristina Pritelli

Usborne Beginners
Caterpillars & Butterflies

Stephanie Turnbull
Illustrated by Rosanna Gasbi

Ballet

Usborne Beginners
Pirates

Catriona Clarke
Illustrated by Greg McLeroy

EGYPTIANS

Stephanie Turnbull
Illustrated by Colin King

Usborne Beginners
Eggs & Chicks

Fiona Patchett
Illustrated by Simon Mendez

Usborne Beginners
ROMANS

Katie Daynes
Illustrated by Adam Larkum

Usborne Beginners
Weather

Catriona Clarke
Illustrated by Kee Feng Chen

Usborne Beginners
Tadpoles & Frogs

Anna Milbourne
Illustrated by Patrizia Donaera

Usborne Beginners
Why do we eat?

Stephanie Turnbull
Illustrated by Tim Haggerty

Usborne Beginners
Under the Sea

Fiona Patchett
Illustrated by Tetsuo Kushii

Usborne Beginners
Bears

Emma Helbrough
Illustrated by Tetsuo Koshi

AZTECS

Trucks

Night Animals

Firefighters

Antarctica

Bugs

COWBOYS

PLANET EARTH

London

Seashore

China

Dangerous Animals

Rainforests

Trees

Bats

Ships

Reptiles

Trains

Knights

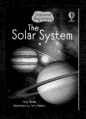
The Solar System

Monkeys

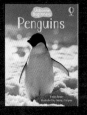
Penguins

Elephants

Tigers

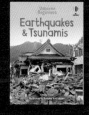
Earthquakes & Tsunamis

Storms and Hurricanes

BEES & WASPS

Wolves

Owls

Snakes